Find, Fetch, Rollover
Dog Tricks

by Gerilyn Bielakiewicz

STERLING INNOVATION
An imprint of Sterling Publishing Co., Inc.

New York / London
www.sterlingpublishing.com

STERLING, the distinctive Sterling logo, STERLING INNOVATION, and the Sterling Innovation logo are registered trademarks of Sterling Publishing Co., Inc.

2   4   6   8   10   9   7   5   3

Published by Sterling Publishing Co., Inc.
387 Park Avenue South, New York, NY 10016
© 2007 by Sterling Publishing Co., Inc.
Distributed in Canada by Sterling Publishing
c/o Canadian Manda Group, 165 Dufferin Street
Toronto, Ontario, Canada M6K 3H6
Distributed in the United Kingdom by GMC Distribution Services
Castle Place, 166 High Street, Lewes, East Sussex, England BN7 1XU
Distributed in Australia by Capricorn Link (Australia) Pty. Ltd.
P.O. Box 704, Windsor, NSW 2756, Australia

Sterling ISBN 978-1-4027-5205-6

For information about custom editions, special sales, premium and corporate purchases, please contact Sterling Special Sales Department at 800-805-5489 or specialsales@sterlingpublishing.com.

TABLE OF CONTENTS

INTRODUCTION

Dogs love to play games with their owners. After all, who wouldn't love all that attention from their loved ones? But how many times have you started playing fetch, only to get bored after a few minutes while your dog kept dropping the ball on your lap insistently? Or perhaps you have one of those dogs who gets distracted before the game really starts. Either way, the trouble could be that one or both of you is bored. Why play the same old games, when you could teach your old (or not-so-old) dog new tricks that will challenge him or her and entertain you?

The *Find, Fetch, Rollover Book & Kit* is intended to help you and your dog have fun together. Whether your dog is old or young, it doesn't matter how much natural talent your dog possesses—if you have the patience and take the time, you truly can teach your dog anything it is physically possible for him or her to do.

Training is a physical skill that you'll get better at with practice. It's all about breaking desired behavior down into small steps that work toward an end goal, and giving the dog clear feedback when he or she has made the correct choices. The tricks and games that follow address a variety of interests and talents, all of which can be accomplished with any dog if you are willing to spend the time to develop a great working relationship.

Raising and living with a dog is a wonderful adventure that we hope you will enjoy even more after playing some of these games. Get ready to spend some quality time with your dog and, most important, have fun!

TRAINING BASICS

CLICKER TRAINING

Whether you are teaching basic obedience or tricks and games, training is a lot more fun and easier for your dog to understand when the instruction is simple and the feedback is clear. The most concise way to convey information while training is through the use of an event marker, or a click, to mark the moment the dog makes the correct choice.

The clicker is a small plastic box with a metal strip inside that, when pressed, makes a clicking sound. We pair this sound with a food reward in the beginning so the click equals a treat! The click is then used to give feedback to the dog about what part of his behavior is rewardable. For instance, if a dog does a lot of barking and we would like to teach him to be quiet, we would click and treat him for taking a breath in between barks. After a few minutes of only clicking and treating for quiet, we would see a dramatic decrease in barking.

Using a clicker to train a dog is a kind and creative way not only to have fun with your dog, but to develop a relationship based on trust, which results in good behavior. The clicker is used to give the dog information or feedback about his behavior on the way to an end goal. The click marks the moment the dog makes the right choice, followed by the food reward. Many folks compare the click to a photograph taken at the exact moment the dog makes a move in the right direction.

When initially introducing the clicker you'll want to click and throw a treat to your dog for five to ten repetitions. Most dogs are quick studies and, after only a few clicks, come to predict that the sound of the click means that food is coming. Once your dog has this reaction, you are ready to begin using the clicker to train and shape behavior.

Some dogs are afraid of the clicker (only about 1 in 100). If this is the case, simply don't click more than once initially. Click once, drop a delicious morsel on the floor in front of the dog, and leave the room. Click and treat in this way every two hours for a day or so, until he is no longer afraid, but instead looks forward to the sound of the clicker because it predicts good things.

When using a clicker and treats to teach a behavior, you must think about what you want the dog to do and break it down into simple steps. You will then click and treat the dog for achieving each step as he progresses toward the end goal. The clicker is used as feedback to let the dog know he is on the right track. Training is flexible, in the sense that we are clicking progress toward an end goal, but if the dog is not progressing forward, we go back to a previously successful step and build up the behavior until the dog is ready to move forward again. When the dog has achieved the steps toward the end goal, we label the behavior and phase out the clicker and treats. Once the dog is offering the behavior regularly, we no longer need the clicker to tell him he chose a rewardable behavior.

THE THREE TOOLS OF TRAINING

LURING

Luring refers to the process of using a treat to guide the dog into the desired position. In clicker training, we would use the treat lure to help guide the dog into position and then use the clicker to mark the moment he arrives in that position, followed by a treat. Remember, it is always click first, then treat. Luring has limited usefulness, in the sense that most dogs become quite dependent on the lure and stop thinking about what they are doing to earn the click. The best way to use a lure in training is to lure for a set number of repetitions (five reps is a good starting place) and then phase it out.

USES

Luring is a limited tool because there is a danger that the dog will become too dependent on the presence of the food lure instead of focusing on the task for which he is getting clicked. When using a lure, you want it to be minimal; do five repetitions with the lure, then try one without it. Go back and forth like this until the dog can perform the behavior reliably without the lure.

RULES

1. Use a food treat as a lure five times in a row and then try one repetition without.
2. When attempting a repetition without the lure, hold your hand as though you still had a treat in it and attempt to direct your dog into position.
3. If your dog performs the behavior correctly without the lure in your hand, click and treat.
4. On the next five repetitions, go back to using a food lure, clicking and treating each one.
5. Now try the next repetition without the lure.
6. If your dog fails to perform the correct behavior, wait a second to give him a chance to figure it out. If he doesn't, be ready with a food lure to help him out.
7. Rotate back and forth between using a food lure and not until your dog is performing the behavior as well with the lure as he did without.
8. Remember, your dog still gets the treat after you click; it is just no longer directly in your hand during the behavior.

Once your dog's performance is just as good without food in your hand, you know you are ready to phase it out completely. Be ready to help your dog with the lure at any point if the behavior begins to fall apart. By being willing to go back to a previous step to help your dog, you are ensuring that he will gain confidence and be able to perform the behavior reliably without help at a later date.

SHAPING

Shaping is the process of breaking a behavior into small, easy steps toward an end goal. Depending on the dog, nearby distractions, and the circumstances, some dogs may need more detailed shaping steps than others. Most trick training involves shaping; by getting good at breaking the behaviors down into little steps, you will find you are quite successful at teaching tricks.

USES

Shaping is used to teach a dog almost anything, from learning to lie down or walk on leash, to being able to retrieve your slippers or a coke from the fridge. This is a skill that you will get better at the more you practice it. The key to shaping is taking small steps, not big leaps, in behavior. The more observant a trainer you are and the more steps you have written in, the more successful your shaping plan will be.

RULES

1. Break down the behavior into small steps and map out a strategy toward the end goal.
2. Click each step for no longer than one to three minutes and then withhold the click to see if the dog attempts to give you more progress in order to earn his click.
3. Remember that shaping is flexible; if you are on the third step but your dog is fooling around or forgets, don't be afraid to go back to a previous step and rebuild the behavior.
4. Expect to go back and rework your strategy, adding more steps or trying a new angle, if your dog gets stuck.
5. Don't click any one step of a behavior for longer than one to three minutes. The longer you stay at one step, the more you are telling your dog that he has arrived at the end goal.
6. Not clicking gives your dog as much information as clicking once the dog knows the game. The absence of a click tells your dog to try something else. Giving your dog a chance to figure things out is important if you are going to become a proficient trainer.

Shaping behavior is one of the most important skills you can attain as your dog's trainer. The better you get at this skill and the more detailed you make your plan, the more quickly your dog will achieve success.

TARGETING

Targeting refers to teaching a dog to touch his nose (or paw, rump, head, belly, etc.) to a target for a click and a treat. The target can be your hand, a yogurt lid, the tip of a pointer, a sticky note, or just about anything.

Uses

Targeting is a form of luring that is used to move a dog toward an object we want him to interact with, move him from one place to another, or guide him into a desired position that can not be accomplished with a food lure. It can be used in general obedience work to teach things like "Go to your bed" and "Come," or in trick work to teach a dog to climb a ladder or push a door closed. Targeting is an invaluable tool in teaching body movements that may not come naturally to some dogs, such as standing on hind legs, backing up, or going backward up the stairs.

Rules

1. Decide upon the body part that is going to touch the target (the nose or a paw is most common).
2. Decide upon a target (your hand, a yogurt lid, a pointer, etc.) Let's use your hand for now.
3. Put a treat between your thumb and the palm of your hand and present it to your dog.
4. When he sniffs it, click and give up the treat.
5. Repeat this five times with the treat under your thumb.
6. On the sixth repetition, present your hand the same way but without the treat under your thumb.
7. If the dog sniffs your hand, click and treat.
8. Do five more repetitions with food under your thumb and then do two without.
9. If your dog is targeting your hand easily, continue without a treat in your hand, but be sure to give the treat after each click.
10. Once your dog is touching your hand with his nose easily, start moving your hand so that he has to get up to follow it.
11. Practice transferring the nose touch on your hand to another object by placing your hand next to the object and click and treat your dog for touching your hand while it is still on the new object.
12. Practice fading your hand by making it smaller (turn it sideways, make a fist, or put your hand palm down or behind the object) until the dog transfers his nose touch to the new object.

Targeting can be made more useful by adding distance or duration to the touch behavior. Adding distance will give you the ability to send the dog away from you to perform the behavior, and duration will enhance the performance of the behavior because the dog will hold the position for longer periods of time.

ADDING DISTANCE TO THE
TARGETING BEHAVIOR

1. Once the dog is easily touching the new target (yogurt lids work great for this), move it several inches away and wait.
2. It may take a second or two, but most dogs will move toward the target to touch it. Click this movement even if the dog doesn't touch the target.
3. We are trying to convey the message that moving toward the target is what we are looking for, so the first several click and treats should be for movement away from you and toward the target.
4. When delivering the treat, it is a good idea to throw the treat in the direction of the target to help encourage the dog to move toward it.
5. After three to five repetitions, withhold the click and wait for the dog to actually touch the target. If he doesn't, move the target back close again and ask him to touch, being sure to time your click for the exact moment he bumps the target.
6. Move the target back out a little and try again. If he moves to the target and bumps it, click and give a jackpot (more than one treat and lots of enthusiastic praise).
7. Keep the target here for three to five more repetitions before moving it further away.
8. Any time you lose the target behavior, bring the target back in close, review for a rep or two, and then move it back out again.
9. As you add distance, don't be tempted to move the target a lot at once, and don't be afraid to move it closer if the dog is having trouble. You will make more progress faster if the dog is confident about what his job is than if you push him too hard.

ADDING DURATION TO THE
TARGETING BEHAVIOR

1. Hold the target in your hand and present it to the dog.
2. Give your cue to target and click and treat each one for five repetitions.
3. Now, withhold the click and observe the dog carefully—you no longer want to click the quick nose pokes, but instead want to wait for and reward the sustained nose touches.
4. Most dogs will touch the target several times and then either do an exaggerated touch or a more prolonged touch. Click either of those, followed by a jackpot (more than one treat and lots of praise).
5. Go back and give your target cue and click and treat the dog for three to five reps, then again withhold the click and wait to see what the dog offers. Click and jackpot any prolonged touches.
6. Repeat this process for a few minutes and then begin to be more picky about what you click. Save the click for the longer touches and ignore the quick ones.
7. This is a bit of a frustrating process for the dog, and most will need you to go back and click and treat them for the target behavior (however quick the touch) every once in a while to build it back up again.
8. Once you are getting prolonged touches with the target in your hand, put the target on the floor and begin again.
9. Once you have prolonged touches with the target on the floor, begin to add distance and duration by moving the target away gradually (see Adding Distance).
10. Don't combine the duration with the distance until the dog can do both well separately. By building each behavior on its own, you ensure the greatest success with very little retraining or remedial work when you combine them later.

These are the tools of training that will help you achieve success in teaching your dog whatever you wish to teach. The more time you spend giving your dog this foundation, the more fun it will be to play the games and perform the tricks that follow. Training sessions should always be short (three to five minutes is ideal), upbeat, and fun. Take frequent breaks to play with your dog to make sure he is having fun!

SIT/STAY

Many dog games and tricks involve your pet sitting and staying while you move something or walk away. These two variations on the basic Sit/Stay—adding duration and handler movement—will make teaching the more interesting tricks a lot easier.

TEACHING SIT/STAY WITH DURATION

1. Lure your dog into a sit with a treat, then click and treat.
2. Once your dog is sitting regularly, delay the click for a beat of two seconds, then click and treat.
3. Gradually mix it up and click on an unpredictable schedule of two seconds, four seconds, two seconds, five seconds, two seconds, eight seconds, three seconds, ten seconds, and so on, until your dog is holding the sit for extended periods of time.
4. If your dog keeps standing up, you are moving too fast. Lower the time between rewarding back down to two seconds for a period of twenty seconds before trying to increase it again.
5. When you can get to ten seconds reliably, call it "Stay" right before you click and treat.

TEACHING SIT/STAY WITH HANDLER MOVEMENT

1. Once your dog is reliable with a simple Sit/Stay, drop the time between rewards down to one or two seconds and move in place. Shuffle your feet, wave your arms, turn in place, bend over, and stand back up.
2. You should be clicking and treating while you are in motion, not when you've stopped. This gives your dog the message to hold his position relative to you no matter what you are doing.
3. As he begins to tolerate you moving in place, begin to take steps away but come right back. If he gets up to follow you, start over with a smaller movement.

FIND

Where's Daddy?

Own a large house and keep
losing your spouse or the kids?
Tired of going to look for a
family member when you are
in the middle of doing
something else? Send your
dog to find them!

This version of the popular childhood game can be played
with your dog as the seeker and your family members as the
hiders. A great way to reward the dog and motivate him to find
you is to show him that you have the Find ball and tease him
with it, then have someone hold his collar while you run off
and hide. The dog must come and find you in gradually more
difficult hiding places. The reward can be a quick game of
fetch when he finds you, followed by another round of hide-
and-seek!

Teaching the Game

1. Decide who will hold the dog gently by the collar.

2. Let the person who is hiding speak to the dog and play with him for ten seconds.

3. Have the holder take the dog's collar while the person hiding makes his or her exit.

4. Release the dog's collar with an excited "Where's (name the person)?"

5. Move slightly in the direction the person hid, but give the dog a chance to lead the way.

6. Act excited and say, "Find Daddy (or other person's name)!" while you slowly move toward the hiding person.

7. If the dog has no clue where to go, have the hider softly call or whistle.

8. When you help the dog, do so only sporadically and try not to help too much.

9. Once the dog finds his person, let them play together for a minute or so and then try again.

10. Include the rest of the family by adding one person at a time and having him or her help the dog at first by calling him sporadically until he finds him or her.

Toy Hide-and-Seek

**Have a small house
that's seriously lacking in
human-sized hiding places?
Can't find a second person to
hide? Hide your pup's favorite
toy and have him seek it instead.**

Explanation

In this alternate version of the hide-and-seek game, your dog is
seeking a favorite toy. The Find ball is a great toy for hiding—
tease your dog with it, then restrain him with a leash or a stay
command while you run off and hide the ball. Once you
return, he can start his search! Conceal the ball in more difficult places as your dog finds it more quickly.

Teaching the Game

1. Try to choose a toy that your dog is crazy for and that has plenty of his scent on it. A Find ball that has been used to play fetch makes a good hiding toy.

2. Show him the toy and tease him with it a bit.

3. Hook his leash to something solid or tell him to stay while you hide the toy.

4. Hide the toy somewhere really obvious at first.

5. Release him with a "Go find it!" and move slowly toward the toy.

6. Once he finds it, get really excited about it and play with it with him for at least a minute.

7. Gradually hide the toy in more difficult places so that he is really using his nose to search.

8. If you have trouble getting your dog excited about toys, try using a toy you can stuff a treat in. Show him the treat before and after you stuff it into the toy and then hide it.

9. Hiding the toy above the dog's head is a more advanced skill for dogs that have mastered searching the floor or ground.

10. Make sure that as you make it harder, you are nearby to encourage the dog and help him be successful. Pointing and verbal "Find it!" clues are allowed as you are teaching your dog this new skill.

Some favorite hiding places might be inside a closet with the door propped open, in your dog's empty food dish, under a towel or blanket, behind the shower curtain, or in a shoe or boot! The possibilities are endless—have fun!

Bobbing For Tennis Balls

A great game to play at your
next barbecue or birthday party!
Invite other dogs to play and
make an outing of it as well!

Explanation

This game is similar to bobbing for apples, except it uses tennis balls instead of apples. It helps greatly if the dog not only loves to fetch but also loves to dunk his head underwater. This game involves filling a shallow container halfway with water and throwing the tennis balls in to float around. The dog must retrieve the tennis balls from the container one at a time. For a larger group, play the game as a relay race, with teams of dogs and handlers and start and finish lines.

Teaching the Game

1. Fill a plastic basin or child's wading pool halfway with water.

2. Show your dog the tennis balls and throw them in the pool one at time.

3. Give your fetch command and encourage your dog to take one of the balls out of the pool.

4. If this is difficult for your dog, use a small basin or bucket at first and fill it almost to the top with water.

5. Put your hand underneath one of the tennis balls and have him retrieve it off your hand.

6. Gradually lower your hand into the water so that he must reach under a bit to get the ball, then click and treat.

7. Once this is going well, take your hand away and encourage the dog to retrieve the ball on his own. This step is harder because the ball floats around a bit and is more difficult to hold on to.

8. Be ready to help by holding the ball so that he can develop confidence.

9. To make this game into a relay race, mark an area the dogs can start from. Put the dunking pool about 15 feet (4 meters) away.

10. One handler and dog from each team race down to the ball pool, retrieve a ball, and race back to their teammates.

11. Once the first pair is back, the next handler and dog do the same until everyone has gone.

12. The first team to finish wins.

This is a great game to play on a hot summer day because everyone is sure to get at least a little bit wet!

The Shell Game

Nosy dogs love this game,
as it gives them a way to get the
news and a nibble all in one
place. Your dog might get so
good at this game that you hire
him out for birthday parties,
bar mitzvahs, and other special
occasions. Who knows, it could
be a new career for you both!

Explanation

Like the old-fashioned sleight-of-hand guessing game, this
game involves hiding a ball under one of three cups and
having the dog use the Push behavior from page 62 to knock
over the cups to find it. For an added wow factor, you can teach
the dog to only knock over the cup with the ball by cueing him
discreetly.

Teaching the Game

1. Teach your dog the Push behavior on page 62. Put your Push behavior on a hand cue, like a pointed finger, by making the gesture, waiting a beat, and saying your verbal cue, "Push."

2. Use the ball to start this since it is the object the dog first learned to push.

3. To transfer the Push behavior from the ball to the cup, have the dog push the ball for three repetitions, then hide the ball and ask him to push the cup.

4. Repeat this for three reps with the ball, then present the cup until he is pushing the cup with purpose. Make sure you click and jackpot (give more than one treat) to accentuate his brilliance.

5. If the pushes are not strong enough, withhold the click until your dog knocks over the cup. By only clicking the pushes that are strong enough to knock over the cup, you will eliminate the ones that don't.

6. Now place the ball under the cup and ask for the Push cue, delaying the click until the dog gives a push strong enough to knock over the cup.

7. Line up the three cups with the ball under one of them. Ask the dog where the ball is. As you indicate each cup, give your pointed finger cue to the cup with the ball and use another gesture to indicate the other cups.

8. When your dog knocks over the correct cup, click and reward him.

Carrier Pigeon

Tired of repeating yourself
to the kids? Maybe they'll listen
to the dog! This game is a great
way to deliver a message without
the nagging. After all, who
wouldn't at least consider
complying with instructions
delivered by a messenger
with four legs and a tail!

Explanation

This game involves giving the dog a piece of paper that he
carries in his mouth and delivers to another person. The Find
ball can be used to keep the message safe and sound.

Teaching the Game

1. Use a sturdy piece of paper initially so the note outlives the slobber.

2. If your dog isn't able to hold onto the paper without chewing it, try securing the note around the Find ball with an elastic band.

3. Hand the note to your dog and ask him to take it. Click and reward for this several times in a row.

4. Next, present the note to the dog, ask him to take it, and then have your helper call him from just a short distance away. Click and treat the dog for moving toward the person.

5. Gradually move the person further and further away, until the dog is searching for the person in another room.

6. Once your helper gets out of sight, have the person call the dog's name or whistle to help him.

7. Once the dog finds the person, the helper can reward the dog with a treat.

The Wind Up

**Your dog will look like
a major league pitching pro
with this fun trick.**

Dog spins in circles with the ball in his mouth as though he is
winding up for the pitch!

Teaching the Game

1. Starting with your dog facing you, use a treat to lure him as far as he will bend in one direction. Click and treat.

2. Each repetition, try to get your dog to reach a bit further, then click and treat. Experiment with each side, as some dogs turn more easily one way then the other.

3. Once your dog can be lured in a full circle, time the click for the halfway point. This will speed up the spin because your dog will be hurrying the rest of the way around to get his treat.

4. Fade the food in your hand by doing five repetitions with food and the sixth without it.

5. Repeat five more with food and two more without.

6. Continue this way until your dog will turn easily, following your hand cue without the food lure. Click in the same spot (the halfway point), with your dog still getting the treat even though it's not in your hand as a lure anymore.

7. Once your dog is spinning easily, fade the hand motion by making an abbreviated one, pausing for a second then making the more exaggerated one.

8. Over the course of a dozen repetitions, be less exaggerated until your dog will spin on the abbreviated cue.

9. Add the Fetch ball in by tossing it to your dog and cueing Spin.

10. Click and treat the halfway point, and celebrate and reward with a short game of fetch.

The Seal Impression

**Get ready to go on
David Letterman! Not only
has your dog proved he has
talent, but now he's doing
impersonations of
other animals!**

Explanation

This trick involves teaching your dog to balance a ball that is
resting on his muzzle. To start with, the dog is in a stationary
position, but if he is particularly talented, he can learn to
balance the ball while walking.

Teaching the Game

1. Ask your dog to sit in front of you and click and treat.

2. Using the hand without the clicker, steady his nose so that it is parallel to the ground. Click and treat. Be sure when you click that the clicker is not right next to his ear, but off to the side or even behind your back. Repeat this step until your dog will allow you to handle his muzzle in this way without pulling away.

3. Hold your dog's muzzle steady and balance the ball on the flattest part of his nose. Depending on how your dog is built, the best place is often at the stop, which is at the bridge of the nose, right in front of the eyes.

4. Once the ball is balanced, click (or have a friend click if you don't have enough hands) and treat for however brief a second the ball remains there.

5. Gradually build the time so that the dog is holding the ball on his nose for a few seconds at a time.

6. Some dogs will lean back as they get tired. If this is the case with your dog, it may be better to have him start in a standing position rather than a sitting position.

7. Ideally, you want to see your dog drop his head and lean forward a bit while keeping his muzzle parallel to the floor. This is the movement that you should click and treat if your dog offers it.

8. Between each click and treat, your dog is going to knock the ball off his nose and you will have to reset it; this is fine.

9. If your dog really likes the ball and wants to play a ten-second game of fetch instead of having a treat, this is also fine.

10. If your dog is particularly talented at this, you may also be able to get him to balance the ball while he moves. Make sure you have the balance behavior down first before you begin to add movement.

Toy Box Targeting

You can't find your keys,
your husband can't remember
where he put his briefcase, and
the kids can never find their
shoes—but at least the dog can
find his ball even if it falls to
the bottom of the toy box.

This trick involves your dog retrieving his Find ball from the
toy basket on command, even if it is buried among other toys.

Teaching the Game

1. Put the Find ball in a shallow basket and click and treat your dog for moving toward it.

2. Once he is offering this easily, delay the click until he dips his nose into the opening.

3. Delay the click again so that he touches the ball with his nose.

4. Ask him to take the ball once he is willingly dipping his head inside the basket.

5. Move the basket further away and try again until he is able to retrieve his ball from the basket when it is across the room.

6. Give the command, "Go find your ball!" just before he dips his head in the basket.

7. Bring the basket back closer to you and add another toy to the basket.

8. Watch your dog carefully and click and treat for retrieving the ball only.

9. As he gets good at this, you can increase the distance again or add more toys to the basket.

10. With practice, you can increase the distance until the basket is just outside the door or, eventually, in another room. You may need to follow the dog and supervise so that he is just retrieving the ball until he gets the hang of it.

Treasure Hunt

Can you dig it? Whether
digging to China or for buried
treasure, your dog can put his
natural talents to good use
with this game that provides
a wonderful outlet for your
dog's digging pleasure.

Explanation

This is a great way to keep an active dog busy and replace
inappropriate digging with a fun game that you can play
together. Find an old sandbox with a lid to use as your digging
pit. Fill the sandbox with sand about 4 inches (10 cm) deep.
Bury the Find ball under the sand and have your dog dig it up!
You can also hide other toys, bones, treats, or whatever will be
fun for your dog to discover.

Teaching the Game

1. Take the Find ball, show it to your dog, and put it right on top of the sand.

2. Encourage your dog to "Get it" and praise him for bringing it to you.

3. Now take the ball and bury it about halfway in the sand and repeat.

4. Gradually bury the ball deeper under the sand until it is no longer visible.

5. Encourage any interest and reward any initial attempts to work harder at getting the ball.

6. If your dog needs help, don't be afraid to uncover the ball a bit and encourage him to put his face deeper into the sand to get the ball out.

7. Some dogs will use their paws to dig the ball out, which is also acceptable.

8. Once your dog is easily digging up the ball, try hiding a second and then a third ball and see if he can get them all out. At first, you may have to help your dog uncover a few of the balls until he catches on to the game.

9. For added entertainment, try putting the balls inside paper lunch bags and burying the bags for the dog to dig up and rip open.

Staying with the treasure hunt theme, be creative with what you hide for your dog to dig up. Paper balls, dry dog cookies, empty ice cream cartons, or yogurt containers all make great discoveries for active young dogs that like to dig!

FETCH

Catch the Bunny

Three little bunnies (who look
suspiciously like tennis balls)
are hopping through the forest
when a dog tries to snatch them
right out of midair. This is a
great way to give an energetic
dog a workout inside or out.

Explanation

This game requires the dog to catch the ball after it has
bounced off the ground at least once. This game should not be
played on a slippery floor, to prevent injury to the dog's back
or legs.

Teaching the Game

1. Get your dog excited about the Fetch ball by teasing him with it and asking him if he's ready.

2. Once you have his interest, give the ball an easy bounce and encourage him to get it.

3. If your dog chases after it at all, encourage him and try to beat him to the ball so he tries to get it faster.

4. Experiment with different bounces at different angles so that your dog can figure out how to grab the ball out of the air.

5. Be patient. This game requires timing on the dog's part, and it takes some dogs a while before they are able to do it.

6. Once your dog is able to grab the ball after the bounce, encourage him to come to you and play fetch with him for a toss or two as the reward.

7. Eventually, bounce three balls to your dog, one at a time, so he can catch each one.

Tag, You're It!

Once your dog can catch
the ball on the bounce, you
can use this skill to play an old
playground favorite. Gather the
family and give everyone a little
exercise while working on your
dog's recall. This might be the
solution if your dog is fonder of
playing keep away than coming
when called once he is in
possession of the ball.

Explanation

This game involves the dog catching the ball on the bounce
and then running to you as fast as he can and tagging your
hand with the ball. You can recruit multiple people to play.

Teaching the Game

1. Teach your dog to target your hand with the ball in his mouth, using the steps in the Training Basics chapter.

2. Bounce the ball and wait for your dog to catch it, and then call him to you, holding out your hand and giving your target cue.

3. Once your dog targets your hand with the ball, click and treat, then bounce the ball for him again as quickly as possible. If you keep the pace rapid, your dog will be more enthusiastic and excited about playing this game with you.

4. Once you bounce the ball, you can take off running so that the dog can chase you down to tag you after he catches the ball.

5. If more than one person is playing, you can scatter yourselves throughout the play area and take turns calling your dog after the catch.

6. After your dog targets the person who is calling him, that person can bounce the ball and another player can call him to come and target.

This is a great way to practice the basic skills of coming when called. Because it is fun, it will give your dog lots of good reasons to come quickly when you call him.

Doggie Basketball

Air Bud, look out! Teach
your favorite canine pal to play
a quick game of one on one.
You'll no longer need to worry
what to do with your energetic
dog on those cold or rainy
days when outdoor exercise
isn't an option.

Explanation

The height of the net will depend on the size of the dog.
Larger dogs can use a kid-size adjustable plastic basketball
hoop and smaller dogs can use a suction cup net stuck to a
sliding glass window or even mounted on top of a small trash
can. The object of the game is to have the dog catch the Fetch
ball and dunk it into the basket.

Teaching the Game

1. Set up the net at a low height and let your dog investigate it.

2. Toss the Fetch ball to your dog and praise him for catching it.

3. After your dog catches the ball, put your hand through the hoop from the bottom and ask him to release the ball to your hand. If he gives it up readily, click and treat.

4. To make it easier for him to figure out what you want at first, you can hold the net in one hand and put your other hand up and through the net to receive the ball.

5. You may want to toss the ball for your dog to fetch so he is coming to drop the ball at speed.

6. Gradually fade your hand in the net so your dog must put the ball in lower to get it in your hand.

7. Once the dog can drop the ball through the rim without much help, mount the net back in position and try again.

8. Keep the net low at first to make it easy for your dog, and be ready to help with a hand in the net if necessary until he figures out what you want.

9. Once he is dropping it in readily, move away from the net so you are not helping him as much, and label the behavior "Dunk it."

10. Practice alternating between tossing the ball to your dog and having him fetch it so he learns that no matter where the ball is, his job is to take it to the net and dunk it.

Play with multiple dogs and have contests as to how many dunks a dog can make in a certain amount of time or which dog can make the most dunks in a row!

Clean Up

**This game is fun for the dog and
useful for the trainer. After all,
who doesn't love a dog that is
willing to pick up after himself!**

In this game, the dog must pick up the balls one at a time and
drop them into a toy box or bucket.

Teaching the Game

1. Use a low-cut box or basket (depending on your dog's height) for the toy box so that it is easy for him to drop the toys in. Place the box between your feet while you are sitting in a chair.

2. Ask your dog to pick up the ball and bring it to you.

3. When your dog gets to you, put your hand out, palm-side up, over the top of the box and ask him to "Drop it."

4. When he opens his mouth to release the ball, click and give him a treat.

5. After several successful repetitions, lower your hand a bit so that it is further into the box and again ask him to release the ball.

6. After several more repetitions, lower your hand to the bottom of the box and ask him to release the ball. Pull your hand away at the last minute so that the ball lands inside the box instead.

7. When this is consistent, use your hand to point inside the box instead of providing a target. Gradually fade where you point by pointing over the box, then inside it, until your dog gets the idea that you want him to put the ball inside the box.

8. Once your dog is picking up the ball and depositing it in the box reliably, you can move the box further away from you. You may have to help him initially by gesturing toward or walking right up to the box to show him what you want.

9. Add more distance as the behavior becomes more reliable.

Jumping Through Hoops

Do you work in an environment full of policies and red tape? Consider making this part of your next presentation at work if your co-workers have a sense of humor and don't mind having a dog around!

Explanation

This game involves getting your dog to jump through a hoop while holding a ball in his mouth.

Teaching the Game

1. Get a child's plastic hula hoop to use as your hoop. Show it to your dog and click and treat him for taking interest in it.

2. For dogs that are afraid of the hoop, try cutting a hole in the hoop to remove the noisemakers, then lay it flat on the ground for your dog to investigate.

3. Click and treat any interest in the hoop. Deliver the treats in the middle or next to the outside rim so your dog begins to associate the hoop with good things.

4. Once your dog is comfortable with the hoop on the ground, begin to hold it off the ground on one side by hand and click and treat any attempts to investigate.

5. Gradually increase the height so it is eventually standing on end while the dog sniffs it.

6. If your dog won't go anywhere near the hoop, lay it back on the ground and use your targeting behavior from the Training Basics chapter to teach him to approach and nose touch.

7. With the hoop standing on one end, click your dog for approaching it and throw the treat through the middle. He may go through the hoop to get his goodie or he may go around—either is acceptable right now.

8. Work in short sessions, using a treat lure if necessary, to get him to approach and step through the hoop. Be sure to click progress toward this end goal—do not just look for the end result.

9. Once your dog is passing through the hoop easily, fade the presence of the treat (no more luring) and wait to click until he is passing through the hoop. The treat can be tossed after the click as your dog finishes passing through the hoop.

10. When your dog is good at this, begin to lift the hoop off the ground a little so he must pick up his feet in order to pass through.

11. Once this is going well, increase the height in small increments until your dog is jumping through without a problem.

12. At this point, you may want to replace the click with a verbal marker like "Yes" and then follow this up with a treat.

13. Once your dog is jumping through the hoop on a regular basis, add the Fetch ball. Throw the ball to your dog. After he catches it, cue him to jump through the hoop and treat when he does.

Gone Hoopy!

**Has dogging it day in
and day out left you tired and
cranky? Play this wacky game
based on the Jumping Through
Hoops trick with your dog
to regain your smile!**

This game involves setting up a small obstacle course with two
small baskets and a hoop. The dog starts near one basket,
retrieves a ball from it, jumps through the hoop, and delivers it
to the other basket. If more than one dog is playing, it can be
run like a relay with two separate courses set up and the dogs
can race to see which one can put all his balls in the basket
first.

Teaching the Game

1. Teach your dog Jumping Through Hoops from the previous page. Start with one ball, hand it to the dog, and have him jump through the hoop.

2. Once he lands, run with him to the other basket and point inside it, asking for "Drop it."

3. If your dog keeps dropping the ball outside the basket, put some sort of target inside the bottom of the basket and have him use his Touch command to nose bop (or ball bop, in this case) the target.

4. Jackpot with more than one treat or a short game of fetch any persistence in getting the ball in the basket.

5. Once he is getting the ball in easily, fade yourself out of the picture by not going all the way to the basket and just pointing. Be ready at first to jump in and help him, but in general move toward getting him to do it more independently.

6. Add the second basket and repeat on the opposite side.

7. Put a ball inside the basket and encourage your dog to retrieve it. If he won't stick his head in the basket, put the ball on your hand and hold it at same height as the rim of the basket. Gradually lower your hand into the basket until it is resting on the bottom.

8. Take your hand away and use a finger to point to the ball and encourage your dog to take it. Gradually offer less help as your dog gets better and better at taking it on his own.

9. Fade out your presence by putting more distance between the basket and you, and see what happens. Be ready to jump in and help if necessary, but the goal is to wean him off the help.

10. Put the whole game together by first practicing the pieces and then adding more steps as the dog begins to catch on.

11. Work up to a point where your dog takes a ball from the basket, runs and jumps through the hoop, and deposits the ball in the other basket. You can start with the baskets just 8 feet (2.5 meters) away from the hoop (or closer for small dogs) at first, and then gradually increase the distance over the course of time.

Army Crawl

Find your inner army recruit as
you crawl around on the floor
with your dog. Fatigues and little
plastic army men are optional.

Explanation

The ball in this game is the grenade, which must be held in the dog's mouth while he crawls under a low obstacle like a coffee table. The dog's job is to go into the minefield (an area scattered with balls), grab a ball (grenade), and crawl under the table to deposit his dangerous cargo in the safe zone on the other side.

Teaching the Game

1. Find a target stick—this can be any type of pointer, but a wooden dowel with a piece of white tape at the end works great.

2. Teach your dog to target the stick with his nose using the steps listed in the Training Basics chapter.

3. Once your dog is nose bopping the stick, ask him to lie down. Present the stick and click and treat any attempt on his part to bop the stick.

4. Gradually move the stick away from your dog, but keep it low to the ground. You want to avoid having your dog stand up to target the stick—instead he should reach forward while lying down.

5. Experiment with where to present the stick so that you get a low wiggle. Click and treat any attempts to touch the stick while remaining in a down position.

6. Once you have a good amount of wiggle, instead of clicking every attempt to target and wiggle along the floor, begin to vary when you click, sometimes waiting for two attempts to wiggle toward the target before you click and treat.

7. Be careful not to make it too hard to earn a click, or your dog will quit on you and start standing up to target the pointer out of frustration.

8. Once your dog is crawling a good distance (about 6 feet or 2 meters), add the Fetch ball to the picture.

9. Give the ball to the dog and ask for down. Praise him for complying and play a short game of fetch.

10. Repeat this step, except this time ask your dog to target as you present the target stick. Click and reward any attempt to target the stick with the ball in his mouth.

11. Move the stick further from the dog as before, until he is crawling a distance of about 6 feet (2 meters) to bop the stick with the ball in his mouth.

12. Once he is confident with this, label the behavior "Crawl" just as you present the target stick. Say, "Crawl," present the stick, and then click and treat any attempt to crawl toward the stick.

13. Once your dog is starting to get it and has begun to crawl on the word "Crawl," begin to fade the target stick. Say the command "Crawl," wait a beat, present the stick, then click and treat the dog for crawling.

14. Over the course of time, you are going to wait longer to present the stick and click and treat any attempt on your dog's part to begin initiating the crawl before he sees the target stick.

15. As your dog begins to get it, fade the target stick by presenting less of it to target so it's further from the ground and more of it is in your hand.

16. Practice getting your dog to crawl under something low like the coffee table by using the target stick at first and then gradually weaning him off of it.

17. Set up the game by littering one side of the coffee table with balls (this is the minefield). The other side is the safe zone and also the starting place.

18. With your dog in the safe zone, send him to get the grenade by saying "Go," "Crawl," then "Take it." He should crawl under the table, grab a ball, and crawl back with it in his mouth. Then he should deposit it on the floor in the safe zone, and go back for the next one.

19. Be ready to walk your dog through each step at first so that he is successful. It's never a problem to help your dog or go back and review a step if he is not getting it.

Stick 'Em Up!

Teach your felonious pooch to surrender to a higher authority in a highly dramatic way. Toy guns and cowboy hats optional!

After stealing the treasure (a ball held in his mouth), the thief is apprehended and forced to surrender. This trick involves the dog holding a ball in his mouth, then rocking back on his rear while sitting and raising his front paws up against his chest.

Teaching the Game

1. Ask your dog to "Sit," then click and treat.

2. Holding the treat in your fist, with one finger extended as a target, present the finger target just above your dog's nose and ask him to "Touch."

3. Click and treat any attempt to tip his head back to touch your finger.

4. Repeat this several times until your dog can do this easily before asking him to follow it a little further back.

5. Delay the click and watch the front feet, clicking and treating the dog for lifting one or both paws up in order to rock back and get the treat.

6. Being able to rock back on his haunches and reach up to touch the target is a skill that most dogs have to build up to gradually. Keep your sessions only one to three minutes long, but make them frequent.

7. If your dog raises entirely up on his hind legs as though dancing, he isn't using the right muscles. Don't click these attempts. Try again, keeping the treat lower and further back rather than straight up.

8. Once your dog can rock back and is bringing both front paws up against his chest easily, delay the click so that he will hold it for a second or two, and gradually build the time.

9. When he has developed enough muscle control to perform the behavior and hold it, fade out the food in your fist and just present your finger as a target. You might do this by presenting your target finger with food in your fist for three reps and do one rep without, until your dog is performing the sit up and beg easily without the food in your hand.

10. Toss the ball to your dog. When he catches it, give your cue and target for Sit Up. Repeat until your dog is catching on and holding the position before you click and play ball as a reward.

11. The cue for Stick 'Em Up can be a gun made by your thumb and pointer. Give this cue, pause a second, then give your target cue. Over several repetitions, fade the target cue so your dog will Stick 'Em Up with just the gun cue.

Dancing with the Dog

**Feel like dancing, but don't have
a partner? Crank up the music
and ask Fido to cut a rug.**

The dog stands on his hind legs and walks backwards. This is a variation of the Stick 'Em Up trick, where the dog sat back on his haunches and raised his paws up against his chest. This variation requires the dog to raise up on his hind legs while holding his front legs either close to his chest or straight out in front. Some dogs will find that pushing their front legs straight out will help with balance, which is also acceptable.

Teaching the Game

1. Ask your dog to "Sit." Using your hand as a target above his head, use your cue to ask him for a nose touch.

2. If he bops your finger with his nose, click and treat.

3. Keep your target hand quite low at first so he only has to lean up to touch it, but gradually make it a bit higher so he needs to stretch up and back to target your hand. Increase the height of the target in tiny increments at first.

4. As you increase the height of the target, pay attention to how your dog is balancing himself. You want to click and treat for rocking back on his rear at first.

5. Later, as you raise the target higher, delay the click, and click and treat your dog for not only raising up to touch the target, but also holding the position for a beat.

6. At this point, you may be clicking for your dog fully extending up on his hind legs to reach the target or rocking back and sustaining a less extended but more controlled pose.

7. As you progress, you should be seeing your dog gain more balance and be able to hold himself on his hind legs for a longer period of time. When he is able to do this, you can then move the target around once he is up on his hind legs and have him follow it by walking a bit on his hind legs.

8. Achieving the muscle strength to be able to walk on hind legs takes time, so be patient and don't practice for too long at any one stretch.

9. Once your dog has achieved height and duration, delay clicking until he can combine both for a split second and work from there to build duration and distance.

Be sure when you are choosing a place to practice that you consider the flooring. A carpet will give your dog far more traction and help him stay balanced, while a tile or linoleum floor may be too slippery.

Catching Flies

Whether your dog's talent for catching flies is of the insect or baseball variety, this skill is invaluable in doggie social circles everywhere!

This classic game requires the dog to catch the ball in his mouth.

Teaching the Game

1. Tease your dog with the Fetch ball and get him interested in it.

2. When he's begging for you to throw it, ask him to sit, then gently lob the ball in his direction.

3. Aim to throw it at him from the side rather than directly in front, as this makes it easier for him to see its path. Most dogs are not very good at catching the ball at first and need lots of tries before they get it right.

4. Make sure your tosses are thrown gently and underhand so that when the ball bonks him on the head it isn't a big deal.

5. Talk to your dog in excited tones and if he misses the ball, race him to it and grab it faster than he can get it so you keep his interest in the ball.

6. Praise any attempt to grab at the ball even if he misses it at first.

7. Once he has a successful attempt, play with him to reinforce his genius by tossing the ball three to four times and letting him chase it down.

Doggie Baseball

This is a great summertime
activity for you and a few doggie
friends. Cook hotdogs and
popcorn and make it a day!

Explanation

This game involves hitting the tennis ball for your dog to catch
or chase down, depending upon which position he is playing.
A second dog can act as a base runner by running around the
bases. For added difficulty, have the runner Sit/Stay at each
base until the handler sends him to the next one. Helpers are
needed to tend the bases and call the dogs and reward them
for staying in position or bringing the ball back to the hitter.

Teaching the Game

1. Set up a baseball diamond with a pitcher's mound, three bases, and a home plate. Station a helper at each of these locations.

2. If there are lot of dogs and handlers playing, several can also be in the outfield.

3. Designate someone to hit the ball. Once he has hit it, the dog on the pitcher's mound should fetch the ball and the handler stationed at first base (or wherever the runner is heading) should call him to tag the base.

4. If there is a runner on first base, the handler at second base should call him to come and Sit/Stay on second base.

5. If the dog with the ball beats the runner to the base, there is one out!

6. If there are dogs in the outfield, handlers stationed out there should encourage the dogs to chase down the ball and run to whichever base is closest to try to tag the runner out.

7. A catch on the fly is an automatic out!

8. Lots of rewards should be given for staying at each base while waiting to run to the next base.

Bombs Away

For the fetching fanatic, nothing is better than picking up and dropping a ball over and over and annoying your fetch partner with your uncanny ability to play keep away at the same time. Put this talent to work by teaching your dog to use this pastime for self-entertainment with a little coaching from you.

Explanation

This trick is a fetching game that involves the use of a deck or porch. The dog drops his ball over the side of the deck or porch, stays while it lands, then runs down the stairs to retrieve it. Once he has it, he goes back up the steps to do it again! If the railings do not allow the dog to stick his head through enough to drop the ball, he can also push the ball off the railing with his nose.

Teaching the Game

1. Once your dog has the Fetch ball in his mouth, show him that you have a delicious treat and wait. When he drops the ball to get the treat, click as soon as he releases it and give him the treat.

2. At first, put your hand right under the ball. Later, fade your hand so your dog is dropping the ball onto the floor.

3. Practice on a set of stairs so that your dog is sitting at the top of the stairs with the ball in his mouth and you are two or three steps down.

4. Ask for "Drop it," and click as he opens his mouth to let go of the ball. If he is reluctant to let go, show him the treat and wait for him to drop the ball for a click and treat.

5. Gradually increase the distance between you so that you are further down the stairs and he is dropping the ball from several steps away.

6. Kneeling next to your dog, take him to the edge of the deck, stick your hand through the railing, and encourage him to drop the ball over the side.

7. When he lets go of it, click and treat, then run with him to fetch the ball and try it again.

8. Gradually fade out the help by not leaving your hand out and not following him to go retrieve the ball. Repeat this over and over, helping him to remember what to do if he is slow to catch on.

9. Add a sit and stay after the drop for added difficulty.

10. Make it a timed event to see how fast he can retrieve the ball after he drops it!

Stair Golfing

Not every dog is allowed
on the golf course, but that
doesn't mean they can't practice
and polish their skills. This
self-entertaining game is great
for a cold winter day when it's
just too icy or cold to go
outside to play.

This is another activity using the ball and stair theme, except
this one is aiming for a hole in one! The dog drops his ball
down a flight of stairs, and sees how many balls he can get into
a basket sitting at the bottom.

Teaching the Game

1. Teach your dog to drop the ball using the steps outlined in the previous game, Bombs Away.

2. Take your dog to the top of a set of stairs and tell him to sit and stay.

3. Sit next to the basket at the bottom of the stairs and cue your dog to drop the ball.

4. If the ball goes in the basket, praise your dog enthusiastically and toss it back for another try.

5. You can use multiple baskets to ensure success.

6. For added exercise, the dog can also retrieve the ball once it hits the bottom.

ROLLOVER

Keep on Rolling! (The Basic Push)

Is your dog nosy? Put that nose to work! Dogs love to investigate by sniffing and pushing things around with their nose. This game provides a great outlet for the nosy dog!

Teach your dog to push the ball with his nose and roll it along. Once the dog knows the basic push and roll, you can turn this into all sorts of fun activities.

Teaching the Game

1. Show your dog the ball and get him excited about it.

2. Put the ball on the floor and when he sniffs it, click and treat.

3. Repeat this five times in a row, clicking and treating each sniff.

4. On the sixth repetition, withhold the click and wait for him to sniff it twice or tap it with his nose, then click and treat.

5. Go back to clicking and treating one sniff on the next repetition.

6. Withhold the click again until you get a more deliberate nose bop, a prolonged sniff, or a nose push, then click and treat.

7. If your dog won't touch the ball with his nose, try enticing him with a dab of peanut butter on the ball. Be sure to click for sniffing or licking.

8. Once your dog is touching the ball on a regular basis, only click for more deliberate nose touches.

9. Continue to experiment every sixth repetition by withholding the click to see if your dog gives a push of the ball with his nose.

10. If he touches the ball but doesn't make much progress pushing it, try putting the ball between you and your dog and offering verbal encouragement.

11. As the distance in pushing improves, introduce the word "Push" by saying it right before your dog's nose touches the ball, then click and treat.

12. Some dogs will use their paws, as well as their noses, to push the ball. This counts as a Push and should be encouraged and rewarded.

13. If your dog tries to retrieve the ball, you are waiting too long to click.

You can experiment with different sizes and types of balls. If picking up the ball becomes a problem, use a larger ball. Beach balls and soccer balls are great substitutes and provide a bigger target for the dog to push.

Doggie Bowling

Who wouldn't want a dog on his or her bowling team? Set up a bunch of bowling pins and let your dog roll for a strike!

The goal of this game is to have your dog roll the ball with his nose and knock down as many pins as possible. You'll need to make a set of bowling pins ahead of time. Emptied plastic soda bottles filled with a small amount of water work great for this. Use 16-ounce or 1-liter bottles for small dogs or 2-liter bottles for larger dogs. The difficulty of the game can be controlled by how much water you put in the bottle.

Teaching the Game

1. Teach your dog to roll the ball with his nose using the steps in the Keep on Rolling game on the previous page.

2. Be sure to set the game up in a long hallway so it's easy for your dog to stay in line with the pins. Set up ten pins in a triangle formation, with four in the back row, three in the next row, two in the next and one in the front.

3. Put the ball about 6 inches (15 cm) in front of pin number one and tell him to "Push." Cheer him verbally and click and treat any contact he makes by pushing the ball into the pins.

4. Repeat and gradually withhold the click for a steadier or longer Push that knocks over the pins.

5. If your dog is intimidated by the pins, set up only one or two at a time and have him practice his Push skill on the pins directly (without the ball) at first to help him figure it out.

6. As your dog gains confidence, move him and the ball further back and see if you can rev him up a bit before dropping the ball on the floor and telling him to "Push."

7. Compete with another dog and keep score of how many pins your dog can knock down in one try.

8. Assign point numbers to the pins or work in an open area for a greater challenge.

9. Use a giant playground ball for Monster Bowling!

Once your dog is having fun and gets the concept of pushing the ball into the pins, you can stop clicking and treating, as the game has become its own reward. If you are adventurous or have a lot of time on your hands, you may want to get together with a few other dog owners and start up a doggie bowling league. Bowling with your dog beats dinner and a movie any day!

Doggie Bowling Three Stooges Style

For those people and dogs with a slapstick sense of humor and a less ambitious approach to dog training, this one's for you!

Explanation

This game is a blast to play with dogs who are confident and have a great sense of humor! The slapstick version of doggie bowling involves a simple Sit/Stay and recall. The pins are set up in a straight line at a halfway point between you and your dog. The dog is on one side of the pin and you and your treats and clicker are on the other. Call your dog to come to you and see how many pins he can knock down by charging through them. This game requires some simple obedience skills that will make the game a bit more organized and fun.

Teaching the Game

1. Set up a single line of pins. In this case, empty ones will fall more easily and help your dog gain confidence.

2. Put your dog in a Sit/Stay on one side of the pins. Step over the line of pins and stand about 6 feet (2 meters) away.

3. Call your dog to you, using a treat to entice him if necessary.

4. Click and treat your dog as he charges through the line.

5. If he stops short and looks worried, try encouraging verbally, by teasing him with the treat, or throwing a ball on your side of the pins. If he is still afraid, go back on his side of the set-up, get him excited with the ball, and then try and race him to go and get it after you throw it over the line of pins.

6. Increase the difficulty of the game by setting up the pins in formation, or adding water to the bottles.

7. Remember that there are some dogs who will love this slapstick game and others that would prefer to remain on the couch. Be respectful of your dog's appreciation of humor. Not all of us are the slapstick type!

8. Invite a group of friends and their dogs to play. Have a contest and see who can knock the most pins down in one charge. Award points for style and creativity! Use different colors of bandannas to designate teams.

Road Kill!

Talented dogs everywhere
will appreciate the finer points
of drama in this version of
playing dead.

For this trick, the dog must lie completely flat on his side without moving, although a slight tail wag adds a little humor and makes it a very cute trick.

Teaching the Game

1. Ask your dog to lie down. Click and treat him for complying.

2. If he is in the typical sphinx position, use a treat held at nose level and moved toward his left or right shoulder to see if you can roll him on to one hip or the other. Most dogs will turn more easily in one direction than another, similar to the way humans are right- or left-handed. Use this to your advantage by rolling your dog onto his dominant side.

3. Start out by clicking and treating any attempt to follow your treat hand with head movement.

4. Gradually get him to reach further and further, until he flops over on one hip or the other.

5. Once he has committed to one hip, attempt to get him to tuck his elbow under him on one side by moving the lure from chin to shoulder in an imaginary line.

6. Click and treat tiny head movements at first until he will follow the treat easily and lie flat on his shoulder.

7. Once he is doing this easily, remove the treat lure from your hand and start over. At first, click and treat any attempt on the dog's part to get into the right position. Move in smaller motions and click and treat his attempts to follow your hand as the target.

8. Go back and forth using food for one or two reps and then one trial without food so that you can begin the process of weaning the dog off of the lure.

9. Practice from the beginning so that the dog is lying down and rolling onto his side, all in one continuous motion. Click and treat any attempts to progress toward the end goal.

10. Gradually fade out having to use your hand gesture by presenting it and fading it as the dog gains confidence of what the task is supposed to be.

Rollover

Mastering this traditional skill is
the first step to impressing your
friends with some of the flashier
Rollover tricks that follow.

Explanation

The dog lies down and rolls over on cue.

Teaching the Game

1. Cue your dog to lie down, and click and treat.

2. Using a treat held at nose level, move it toward your dog's shoulder. You may find your dog turns more easily one way than another. If so, always move the treat in this direction.

3. Click and treat your dog for following the treat with his nose.

4. Don't try to get him to turn further than he can easily offer at first. Click and treat at the point of resistance, where he is extending his neck, but not struggling to reach the treat.

5. Repeat this multiple times from the start until he turns easily onto one hip.

6. Using the treat as a lure, encourage him to reach further until he follows the treat by rolling onto his back. Always start with the lure in front of your dog to help him gain momentum.

7. Continue to lure him until you can get him to roll all the way over easily. Not all dogs find this an easy task, so be patient and break it down into easier steps if your dog is having trouble.

8. Once your dog is rolling over easily, fade the lure by taking it out of your hand. You should still be clicking and treating, but since he is easily rolling over, you are now clicking at the point that he is on his back and then delivering the treat when he completes the roll.

Pig Roast Impression

Did someone say "Luau"?
Fat dog optional!

The dog lies belly-down on the floor with his chin resting on the floor between his paws and the ball in his mouth. If he cooperates, he will look very much like a roasted pig with an apple in its mouth at a Hawaiian Luau!

Teaching the Game

1. Cue your dog to lie down. As soon as he hits the floor, click and treat.

2. Click and treat every two seconds for one minute to encourage him to lie still.

3. Next, delay the click until your dog is waiting three to five seconds between clicks and treats.

4. Gradually increase the time to ten seconds between rewards.

5. Delay the click again and watch your dog carefully. Click and treat any head movement and deliver the reward on the floor between his paws.

6. As your dog starts to offer more head movement, delay the click until he puts his chin on the floor. Click and treat this chin to the floor motion for one minute.

7. Withhold the click now and watch closely for him to hold his chin to the floor for a second longer than before, then reward.

8. Gradually increase the difficulty by only clicking and treating your dog for resting his chin for a second or more at a time.

9. Once your dog is offering this on a regular basis, add the Rollover ball. Throw the ball to your dog. After he catches it, cue him to lie down and click and treat when he does.

10. Withhold the click and wait for head movement, then click and treat.

11. Withhold the click and wait for his chin to touch the floor between his paws. Reward.

12. Build the time slowly by delaying the click until he leave his chin on the floor for longer periods of time (two or three seconds).

13. Label the behavior "Pig roast," then cue the down and wait. Click and treat only the long chin touches.

14. Fade out the down cue by putting more time between saying "Pig roast," the new cue, and "Down," the old cue.

Pig on a Spit

A deluxe version of
the Pig Roast Impression,
this trick is guaranteed to
amuse your friends.

This is an expanded version of Pig Roast in which the dog
must not only lie down with the ball in his mouth, but rollover
like a pig on a spit as well. The trick has more entertainment
value if the dog can do this multiple times in a row.

Teaching the Game

1. Teach your dog the basic Rollover, from page 70.

2. Toss the Rollover ball to your dog and cue Down. Click and treat when he lies down.

3. Repeat this two or three times, then as soon as your dog lies down, cue him to rollover.

4. Click and reward (throwing the ball for a toss or two is fine) any attempt to begin to rollover.

5. Once your dog is initiating the rollover, wait until he is on his back before you click. This will speed up the rollover and help him keep his balance and his hold on the ball.

6. If your dog won't rollover with the ball in his mouth, go back and practice Rollover without it and then add the ball back in and try again.

Pig in a Blanket

Whether hiding from
the cold on a winter day, or
from his owners after a mistake
on the rug, every dog will find
a use for this trick!

This trick involves the dog lying down on a blanket, grabbing
the corner in his mouth, and rolling over while holding it,
essentially rolling himself up in the blanket.

Teaching the Game

1. Teach your dog the Rollover behavior on page 70.

2. Lay an unfolded towel or blanket flat on the floor and ask your dog to lie down on it. You may want to practice this trick on a soft surface, which will be more comfortable for the dog.

3. Bunch up one corner so it is easy to grab, and tell your dog to "Take it." Click and treat your dog for any attempt to grab the blanket.

4. Once he has this step down, work on rolling over separately by cueing him to lie down and rollover on the blanket. You may have to help him at first by encouraging your dog to lie on the blanket by pointing or gesturing.

5. Combine the two steps by telling him to take the corner and immediately giving your cue to rollover. This is a behavior chain, and each behavior in the chain must be strong in order for the dog to be able to put it together and do the behavior fluently.

6. When asking him to take the corner and rollover in succession, you should initially click any attempt to start the roll once he has grasped the edge of the blanket. You will no longer be clicking each behavior individually, but instead cueing "Take it" and clicking and treating the dog for beginning to rollover. (In the beginning, if you wait to reward the whole behavior chain at once, the dog will get confused and quit.)

7. As he gets good at this and is offering to begin the rollover, gradually delay the click until he is further into the rollover position. This will speed up the rollover and give you the end result you want.

8. If you are having trouble with the entire performance, separate out the two behaviors—take it and rollover—and practice them separately until the dog is consistent before asking for them together again.

Ball Racing

Who says a dog can't
participate in leisure activities?
This is the ultimate in canine
entertainment! It's Find, Fetch,
and Roll (balls) Over, all
rolled into one!

Explanation

The dog retrieves all three balls and drops them in a line at the
top of a staircase. The handler cues the dog to push each ball
over the edge in rapid succession and keeps track of which ball
gets to the bottom of the stairs first. The dog then retrieves all
three balls, one at a time, and starts the game again. For added
fun, a basket can be placed at the bottom of the stairs and
points can be awarded for getting the ball into the basket. If
multiple dogs are playing, one dog can be at the bottom of the
stairs retrieving the balls while the dog at the top pushes them
down the stairs.

Teaching the Game

1. Sit at the top of a set of stairs and have your dog retrieve one ball at a time and bring each one back to you.

2. Help your dog line up the balls along the top step by indicating with your finger or a small piece of masking tape where he should drop each ball.

3. Using your Push command, get your dog to push each ball so it rolls down the stairs. Encourage your dog to push one after another without pause by delaying your click and treat until the last push.

4. Once the last ball hits the bottom, tell him to fetch and have him retrieve the balls one at a time to start the game again.

5. If you are playing with two dogs, the dog at the bottom should wait until all the balls have reached the bottom before he begins to retrieve them and bring them back to the top. This version is great to play with a tired old dog and an exuberant youngster working as a team!

Wrap Up

We hope you've enjoyed teaching
these tricks and games and
have had fun with your dog.
Remember that training a dog is
a lifelong affair based on a good
relationship and lots of practice.
Dogs are wonderful examples of
living life in the moment—give
them the tools to do so and
you'll both be rewarded!